To Doug:
Love Mam -
" Happy Cooking "
Christmas 1993 -
x x x.

ORIENTAL
COOKING

Photography by Peter Barry
Designed by Richard Hawke and Claire Leighton
Edited by Jillian Stewart and Kate Cranshaw
Recipes by Judith Ferguson, Lalita Ahmed and
Jacqueline Bellefontaine

3448
© 1993 Coombe Books
This edition published in 1993 by Coombe Books
for Parragon Book Service Ltd.,
707 High Road, Finchley, London N12 0BT
All rights reserved.
Printed in Hong Kong
ISBN 1-85813-366-1

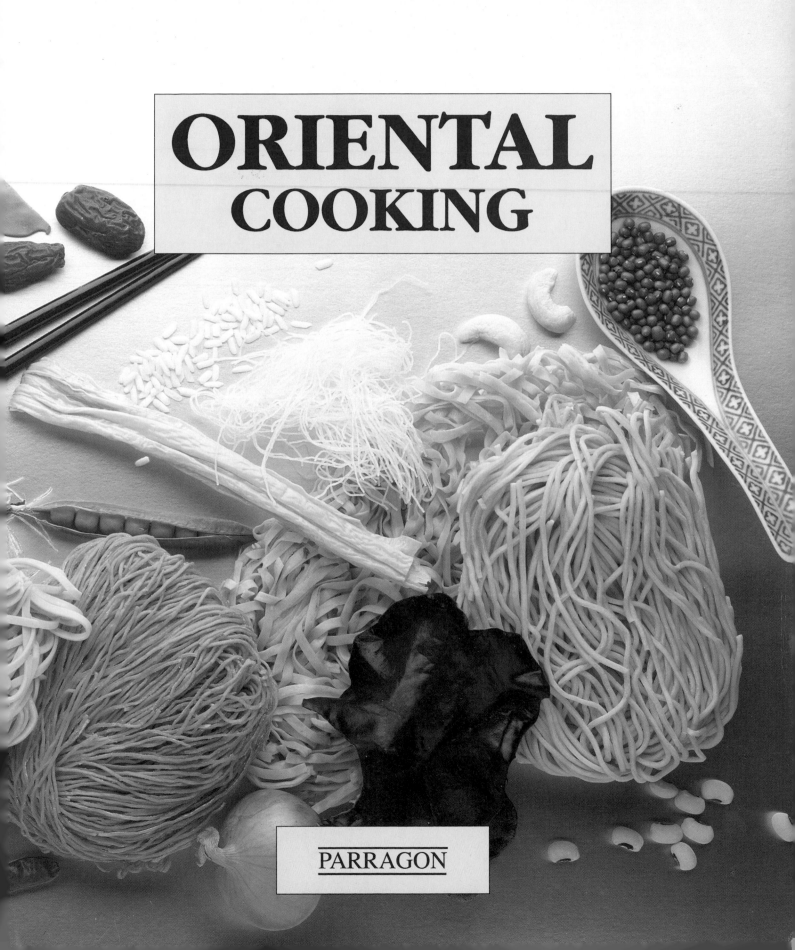

ORIENTAL
COOKING

PARRAGON

Contents

Introduction

The East has been a subject of fascination to the West for centuries. Now, as greater numbers of people visit these far away places their various cuisines are becoming increasingly popular. Indian and Chinese cuisines are familiar to most of us, but Japanese, Thai, and Indonesian foods have only recently become popular.

China and India are the main influencing elements in Oriental cuisine and in many Far Eastern countries such as Thailand, Indonesia and Malaysia this is quite apparent. Indian spices are used in curries and these blend with Chinese ingredients and cooking methods to produce a cuisine which is a diverse mixture of tastes. In contrast, Japan has taken little from the rest of the East, or anywhere else, and its cuisine is very much entwined with its philosophy of harmony and balance. The food is delicate, simple and elegant with an emphasis on clean sharp natural tastes and freshness. Thai food, on the other hand, is a mass of flavours, textures and colours all mingled together. Small hot chillies are a favourite ingredient, quite often along with coconut milk, fish sauce and shrimp paste. Another Thai favourite is fresh coriander of which the roots and stems are used as much as the leaves.

Malaysian food is a blend of mildly flavoured Chinese dishes with a splash of curry powder or chilli and Indian spices which are used in Malay-style curries. Chillies are used with great zeal; with lemon grass, tamarind, shrimp paste, galangal, turmeric and coconut being the other most commonly used flavourings. Indonesian cuisine is another favourite and consists of thick aromatic curries, spicy *sates* (satays) with peanut sauce, pickled fish, chilli spiced foods, many offal based dishes, and good use of fruit and vegetables.

As Indian and Chinese cuisines have become so popular, most of the ingredients for preparing these dishes are available in large supermarkets. Some of the ingredients for the Thai and Indonesian recipes may be more difficult to obtain, but these can normally be found in Oriental stores or from specialist mail order companies. Alternatives for these ingredients have been given where possible, although the resulting dishes will not taste quite as authentic they should.

Oriental cooking is great fun, with many new tastes and combinations of ingredients to excite the palate and please the eye. Quantities of spices and chillies do not have to be strictly adhered to, and once you have mastered the art of Oriental cooking and have a feel for the tastes and combination of ingredients, you can start to experiment with some new dishes of your own.

SPICY VEGETABLE SOUP

Use the vegetables suggested in whatever proportions you like to make this tasty soup.

SERVES 4

450g/1lb mixture of:
Carrots cut in short strips
Chinese leaves, coarsely shredded
Spinach, stalks removed, washed and
    leaves coarsely shredded
Mange tout
Bamboo shoots, thinly sliced
Bean sprouts

1 litre/1¾ pints water
4 shallots, finely chopped
¼-½ tsp sambal ulek
1 small piece lemon grass, peeled and the
    core chopped
2 curry leaves or bay leaves
1 tsp muscovado or dark brown sugar
220ml/8 fl oz coconut milk
Small handful fresh coriander leaves, stems
    removed
Salt and pepper

1. Prepare the vegetables as directed.

2. Combine water, shallots, sambal ulek, lemon grass, curry leaves or bay leaves and sugar in a large, heavy-based pan.

3. Partially cover and simmer for 15-20 minutes.

4. Add the carrots and after 5 minutes add remaining vegetables in the order given, allowing the bean sprouts to cook for 2 minutes only.

5. Add the coconut milk and coriander leaves and allow to simmer gently for about 5 minutes.

6. Add salt and pepper to taste and serve immediately.

TIME: Preparation takes about 20 minutes, and cooking takes 25-30 minutes.

BUYING GUIDE: Sambal ulek is a paste of dried chillies and salt and can be bought at some supermarkets and Oriental stores.

CHICKEN AND SWEETCORN SOUP

This soup uses baby corn on the cob and chicken and is flavoured with ginger and soy sauce.

SERVES 4

180g/6oz canned sweetcorn
700ml/1¼ pints chicken stock
2 cooked chicken breasts
12 baby corn on the cob
2.5cm/1-inch piece of fresh ginger root, chopped
2 tbsps light soy sauce
Pinch monosodium glutamate (optional)
Few drops chilli sauce
Salt and pepper

1. Place the canned sweetcorn in a food processor with 120ml/4 fl oz of the chicken stock. Process until smooth.

2. Strain the purée through a sieve, pushing it through with the help of a spoon.

3. Cut the chicken into thin slices and stir them into the remaining stock, in a saucepan.

4. Stir in the sweetcorn purée.

5. Add the baby corn and bring to the boil. Simmer for 15 minutes. Add the ginger, soy sauce, and monosodium glutamate. Continue cooking for another 10 minutes.

6. Add a few drops of chilli sauce. Check the seasoning, adding salt and pepper if necessary and serve.

TIME: Preparation takes about 5 minutes and cooking takes approximately 25 minutes.

COOK'S TIP: Prepare the soup the day before serving to give the flavours time to develop.

VARIATION: Use canned creamed corn instead of processing corn kernels.

LEMONY FISH SOUP

A lemon flavoured fish soup makes a delicious start to a meal.

SERVES 4

900g/2lbs sole or plaice fillets, skin and
    bone reserved
1.5 litres/2½ pints water
3 black peppercorns
1 curry leaf or bay leaf
Juice of 1 lemon
2 tbsps oil
4 shallots, thinly sliced
1 clove garlic, crushed
1 small piece ginger, thinly sliced
1 small piece tamarind, soaked in 60ml/4
    tbsps hot water
1 small piece lemon grass, peeled and the
    core chopped
1 small bunch kuchai or chives, snipped
4 tomatoes, skinned, seeded and diced
Salt and pepper

1. Combine the fish bones and skin with water, peppercorns, curry leaf or bay leaf and lemon juice in a deep, heavy-based saucepan.

2. Partially cover and bring to the boil. Lower the heat and simmer gently for 15 minutes. Strain the stock immediately and set aside.

3. Cut the fillets into small pieces and reserve.

4. Heat the oil in the rinsed-out pan and cook the shallots, garlic and ginger until soft.

5. Strain on the soaking liquid from the tamarind and add the strained fish stock.

6. Add the reserved fish fillet pieces and lemon grass to the pan. Simmer for 10-15 minutes or until the fish is cooked.

7. Add the kuchai or chives and tomatoes to heat through. Season with salt and pepper and serve.

TIME: Preparation takes 20 minutes and cooking takes 30-35 minutes.
BUYING GUIDE: Kuchai are also sold as Chinese chives.

BEEF AND NOODLE SOUP

Marinated beef is sliced and cooked in beef stock with noodles to make a rich and extremely filling soup.

SERVES 4

225g/8oz fillet of beef
½ tsp chopped garlic
1 spring onion, chopped
2 tbsps soy sauce
Salt and pepper
225g/8oz fresh noodles
Few drops sesame oil
700ml/1¼ pints beef stock
Few drops chilli sauce
1 tbsp chopped chives

1. Cut the beef into thin slices. Sprinkle the chopped garlic and spring onion over the meat. Finally, sprinkle over the soy sauce and season with salt and pepper. Marinate the meat for 15 minutes.

2. Cook the noodles in boiling, salted water to which a few drops of sesame oil have been added. Rinse them in cold water and set aside to drain.

3. Bring the beef stock to the boil and add the beef and the marinade. Simmer gently for 10 minutes.

4. Stir in the noodles, season with a few drops of chilli sauce and simmer just long enough to heat the noodles through.

5. Serve with chives sprinkled over the top.

TIME: Preparation takes about 5 minutes, plus 15 minutes marinating time and cooking takes approximately 12 minutes.

VARIATION: If you use a marrowbone to make the stock, add a little chopped beef marrow to the soup, just before serving.

WATCHPOINT: Do not overcook the noodles; they should still be quite firm at the end of Step 2.

SPICY CHICKEN AND PRAWN SOUP WITH LIME AND EGG

King prawns, spices, chicken and peanut butter make a delicious combination in this soup.

SERVES 4

1.4 litres/2½ pints water
6 raw, unpeeled king prawns
1kg/2¼lbs chicken pieces
2 curry leaves
Salt
4 shallots, finely chopped
1 clove garlic, crushed
2 tsps fresh root ginger, grated
1 tsp ground coriander
¼ tsp cayenne pepper
1 tbsp crunchy peanut butter

1 sliced hard-boiled egg, 1 thinly sliced
    lime, and celery leaves to garnish

1. Combine water, prawns, chicken, curry leaves and salt in a large, heavy-based saucepan.

2. Bring to the boil and then simmer until prawns are pink.

3. Remove the prawns and set aside.

4. Continue simmering until the chicken is cooked. Remove chicken, strain and reserve the stock.

5. Skin and bone the chicken and cut the meat into thin shreds.

6. Peel the prawns and slice in half lengthwise.

7. Pour the stock into the rinsed-out pan and add the shallots, garlic, ginger, spices and peanut butter.

8. Bring to the boil and simmer, uncovered, for 15 minutes.

9. Add the chicken, prawns, and cook a further 2 minutes to heat through.

10. Garnish individual servings with the egg and lime slices and celery leaves.

TIME: Preparation takes about 15 minutes and cooking takes 20-25 minutes.

BUYING GUIDE: Curry leaves can be bought at Oriental stores.

Sweet and Sour Pork Satay

Satays make an excellent starter to a meal or make an appetizing change to the usual barbecue fare.

SERVES 4

450g/1lb lean pork cut into 1.25cm/½-inch pieces

Marinade
1 small piece tamarind soaked in 60ml/ 4 tbsps hot water, then sieved
1 tbsp dark brown sugar
1 small onion, finely chopped
90ml/6 tbsps soy sauce
2 tsps grated fresh root ginger
¼ tsp ground nutmeg
¼ tsp ground coriander
Pepper

Sauce
Reserved marinade
2 tbsps tomato purée
140ml/¼ pint coconut milk
Juice of 1 lemon

Tomato wedges or pieces of fresh pineapple to garnish

1. Put the pork cubes into a deep bowl. Combine the marinade ingredients and pour half over the pork. Leave to marinate in the refrigerator for 30 minutes.

2. Thread the pork cubes onto thin bamboo skewers and place on a barbecue grill or under a pre-heated grill.

3. Cook for 8-12 minutes, turning frequently, until the pork is golden brown and tender. Baste frequently with the marinade during cooking.

4. Combine the reserved half of the marinade and any remaining marinade left from basting the pork together with the tomato purée and coconut milk.

5. Bring gently to the boil and allow to simmer for about 10 minutes to reduce. Stir in the lemon juice.

6. Serve the satay on a bed of rice and spoon over some of the sauce. Serve the remaining sauce separately and garnish the plate with tomato wedges or fresh pineapple.

TIME: Preparation takes 30 minutes, including marinating, cooking takes 18-23 minutes.

PREPARATION: Cooking time will depend on the power of the grill used.

INDONESIAN VEGETABLE OMELETTE

Kuchai or Chinese chives are a member of the onion family, which when cooked, have a wonderful garlic and onion flavour.

SERVES 4

½ small aubergine, halved lengthways
1 canned whole bamboo shoot, diced
½ red pepper, diced
2 tbsps vegetable oil or butter
Few kuchai or chives, snipped
¼ tsp ground nutmeg
¼ tsp ground cumin
Pinch cayenne pepper
6 eggs
Salt

1. Lightly score the surface of each half of the aubergine and sprinkle with salt.

2. Leave to stand 30 minutes to draw out any bitter juices. Rinse very well and pat dry.

3. Cut the aubergine into dice the same size as the bamboo shoot and red pepper.

4. Heat the oil or butter in a heavy frying pan and add the aubergine, bamboo shoot and red pepper. Stir-fry until slightly softened, then remove half of the vegetables and set them aside.

5. Beat the kuchai and spices with the eggs and salt.

6. Pour half the egg mixture into the pan over the vegetables and cook over a moderate heat until set and lightly browned on the bottom.

7. Carefully turn the omelette over and brown the other side, remove from the pan and keep warm on a serving plate. Make another omelette with the remaining ingredients and cut into wedges before serving.

TIME: Preparation takes 30 minutes, including standing time and cooking takes about 20 minutes.

BUYING GUIDE: Canned whole bamboo shoots can be bought from Oriental stores. If unavailable use sliced bamboo shoots.

CHICKEN OR TURKEY PAKORAS

These delicious pakoras can be made with cooked as well as raw meat and it is therefore an excellent and unusual way to use left over Christmas turkey or Sunday roast. Raw chicken breast has been used for the recipe below, as it is more succulent than cooked meat.

SERVES 6-8

150ml/5 fl oz water

1 medium onion, coarsely chopped

2-3 cloves garlic, coarsely chopped

1-2 fresh green chillies, coarsely chopped; remove the seeds if you prefer a mild flavour

2 tbsps chopped coriander leaves

125g/5oz besan or gram flour (chick pea flour), sieved

1 tsp ground coriander

1 tsp ground cumin

½ tsp garam masala

½ tsp chilli powder

1 tsp salt or to taste

Pinch of bicarbonate of soda

340g/12oz fresh, boneless and skinless chicken or turkey breast

Oil for deep frying

1. Put 90ml/3 fl oz water from the specified amount into a liquidiser followed by the onion, garlic, green chillies and coriander leaves. Blend until smooth. Alternatively, process the ingredients in a food processor without the water.

2. In a large bowl, mix the besan, coriander, cumin, garam masala, chilli powder, salt and bicarbonate of soda.

3. Add the liquidised ingredients and mix thoroughly.

4. Add the remaining water and mix well to form a thick paste.

5. Cut the chicken into pieces and gently mix into the paste until the pieces are fully coated.

6. Heat the oil over medium heat; when hot, using a tablespoon, put in one piece of besan-coated chicken at a time until you have as many as the pan will hold in a single layer without overcrowding it. Make sure that each piece is fully coated with the paste.

7. Adjust heat to low and fry the pakoras for 10-15 minutes turning them over half way through. Remove the pakoras with a perforated spoon and drain on kitchen paper.

TIME: Preparation takes 20 minutes, cooking takes 30 minutes.

SERVING IDEAS: Serve with tomato chutney or the chutney of your choice.

PRAWNS IN NORI PACKAGES

*These seaweed wrapped prawns make a delicious starter to a meal, if wished,
prepare a double quantity of sauce and use some for dipping.*

SERVES 3-4

12 king prawns
3 square nori
12 chives

Grilling sauce
90ml/6 tbsps soy sauce
3 tbsps mirin
3 tbsps grated ginger squeezed for juice

1. Shell and de-vein the prawns, but leave on the tail ends.

2. Pass the sheets of nori over a gas flame or steam on both sides to freshen.

3. Cut each into 4 strips. Mix all the sauce ingredients together and brush over the prawns.

4. Brush the nori strips and wrap one around each prawn, but do not completely cover.

5. Place under a pre-heated grill and cook for 1 minute on each side, brushing with the remaining sauce.

6. Tie each with 1 chive.

TIME: Preparation takes about 20 minutes and cooking takes about 2 minutes.

BUYING GUIDE: Nori is a type of seaweed which is sold in thin sheets.

FRIED PARCELS

Serve these crispy parcels with a spicy sauce to dip them into.

MAKES 48

225g/8oz Wonton wrappers
1 egg white
Oil for deep frying

Filling
2 tbsps oil
120g/4oz raw, shelled peanuts
2 cloves garlic, crushed
225g/8oz shelled prawns, roughly chopped
1 piece ginger, grated
1 tbsp soy sauce
2 eggs
8 spring onions, finely chopped
Salt and pepper

1. Heat the oil for the filling in a small frying pan. Chop the peanuts finely and add to the oil.

2. Cook over moderate heat, stirring often, until light brown.

3. Add the crushed garlic and continue to cook until the peanuts are golden brown.

4. Allow to cool and combine with the other filling ingredients.

5. Place about 1 heaped teaspoon of the filling on to each wonton wrapper.

6. Brush the edges with lightly beaten egg white and fold over to make a triangle.

7. Seal the edges well and repeat with the remaining wrappers and filling.

8. Heat the oil for deep-frying in a wok or deep fat fryer, and when hot fry a few parcels at a time for 2-3 minutes or until crisp and golden brown. Drain on kitchen paper and serve hot.

TIME: Preparation takes 20 minutes and cooking takes 2-3 minutes per batch.

BUYING GUIDE: Wonton wrappers can be bought fresh or frozen from Oriental stores.

VEGETABLE TEMPURA

These make a delicious starter or excellent finger food for a party.

SERVES 4

Selection of the following ingredients prepared as directed:

Mushrooms, whole fresh

Green peppers, cut in 5mm/¼-inch thick rings or strips

Onions, cut in 5mm/¼-inch rings

Asparagus tips

Mange tout, ends trimmed

French beans, ends trimmed

Courgettes, halved lengthwise and then cut across into thin slices

Okra, stems removed and pods left whole

Cauliflower and broccoli, cut into florets

Sweet potato, peeled and sliced into ½-inch rounds

Carrots, peeled and cut into diagonal slices

Cucumber, quartered lengthwise and cut into 2.5cm/1-inch wedges

Oil for frying

Dipping sauce

120ml/4 fl oz chicken stock

60ml/4 tbsps soy sauce

60ml/4 tbsps sherry or sake

Pinch sugar

Small piece daikon radish, grated

Small piece ginger, grated

Batter

1 egg yolk

280ml/½ pint iced water

120g/4oz plain flour

1. Prepare the vegetables as directed.

2. Mix all the ingredients for the sauce except the radish and ginger. Pour the sauce into 4 small bowls.

3. Place a small mound of grated radish and one of grated ginger on each of 4 plates.

4. Heat oil in a deep-fat fryer to 350°F/180°C.

5. Beat the egg yolk lightly and beat in the water. Sift in the flour and stir with a table knife. The batter should look lumpy and under-mixed.

6. Dip each vegetable in the batter and shake off the excess. Lower ingredients carefully into the hot oil and cook for about 2 minutes, turning once or twice.

7. Fry only 3 or 4 pieces at a time and fry only 1 kind of vegetable at a time. Do not coat too many vegetables in advance.

8. Drain fried vegetables on kitchen paper on a rack for a few seconds before serving.

9. Serve while still hot and crisp. Each person may mix a desired amount of the grated radish and ginger into the dipping sauce to eat with the tempura.

TIME: Preparation takes 30 minutes and cooking takes 2 minutes per batch.

COOK'S TIP: Do not over mix the batter.

IMPERIAL PORK ROLLS

These fried rice paper rolls are stuffed with a mixture of bean sprouts, black mushrooms and pork and served with a spicy fish sauce.

SERVES 4

½ tbsp vinegar
1 tbsp water
1 tbsp fish sauce
1 tsp sugar
½ tsp chopped fresh ginger root
Chilli sauce
4 dried Chinese black mushrooms, soaked for 15 minutes in warm water
340g/12oz boned pork shoulder, very finely chopped
½ tsp oil
120g/4oz bean sprouts, blanched and drained
1 tbsp soy sauce
½ tsp cornflour
Salt and pepper
16 sheets rice paper, soaked in warm water for 10 minutes
A little beaten egg
120ml/4 fl oz oil

1. To make the sauce, mix together the vinegar, water, fish sauce, sugar and ginger and allow to stand for 30 minutes. Add a few drops of chilli sauce, just before serving.

2. Dice the mushrooms very finely and mix them with the meat.

3. Heat the ½ tsp oil in a wok and stir-fry the above together with the bean sprouts, soy sauce and cornflour for 2 minutes. Allow to cool. The mixture should be quite dry. Add salt, pepper and chilli sauce to taste.

4. Drain the rice paper sheets and spread them out on your work surface. Place a little of the cooled stuffing in the centre of each sheet, roll it up and seal the edges with a little of the beaten egg.

5. Heat the 120ml/4 fl oz oil in a wok and fry the rolls gently on all sides, beginning with the sealed side. Drain on kitchen paper.

6. Serve the rolls hot, with the sauce in individual bowls.

TIME: Preparation takes about 30 minutes and cooking time is approximately 15 minutes.

SERVING IDEAS: Serve the rolls with lettuce leaves and fresh mint. Guests should wrap the mint and lettuce leaves around the rolls, before dipping them into the sauce.

BUYING GUIDE: These rice paper sheets are round and can be bought, in packets, from Oriental stores.

PRAWN EGG CUSTARD

These savoury custard cups make an unusual start to a meal.

SERVES 4

Stock
570ml/1 pint dashi
1 tsp soy sauce
1 tsp mirin
Pinch salt

5 eggs, beaten
30g/1oz bean sprouts
4 king prawns, peeled
4 mange tout blanched and cut in half
4 dried shiitake mushrooms, soaked 30
    minutes, drained and scored

1 piece grated pickled ginger to garnish

1. Bring stock ingredients to the boil. Take off the heat and leave to cool.

2. Strain the stock and when cool mix with the beaten eggs.

3. Divide the mixture evenly among 4 heat-resistant cups or small bowls.

4. Add the bean sprouts and position the prawns so the tail shows.

5. Add the mange tout and float a mushroom on top of the custard.

6. Pour water into a steamer or a large, deep saucepan and bring to the boil. Place the cups on a steamer or a rack above the boiling water.

7. Cover the pan or steamer and cook over high heat for about 2 minutes. Reduce the heat and steam until just set, about 15 minutes.

8. Garnish with the pickled ginger.

TIME: Preparation takes 20 minutes and cooking takes about 20 minutes.

COOK'S TIP: Dashi is the principal stock used in Japanese cooking and is made from dried fish flakes and kombu seaweed. It is sold in packs or as instant granules in Oriental stores.

GADO GADO

The peanut sauce that accompanies this salad is similar to that served with satay.

SERVES 4

1 tbsp oil
1 carrot, peeled and cut into thin strips
1 potato, peeled and cut into thin strips
120g/4oz French beans, trimmed
120g/4oz Chinese leaves, shredded
120g/4oz bean sprouts
½ cucumber, cut into thin strips

Peanut sauce
2 tbsps oil
60g/2oz raw shelled peanuts
2 red chillies, seeded and finely chopped
2 shallots, finely chopped
1 clove garlic crushed
140ml/¼ pint water
1 tsp soft brown sugar
Juice of ½ lemon
90ml/3 fl oz coconut milk
Salt

Sliced hard-boiled eggs and cucumber
    sliced or cut into strips to garnish

1. Heat a wok and add oil. When hot add the carrot and the potato. Stir-fry for 2 minutes then add the beans and Chinese leaves.

2. Cook for a further 2 minutes and add the bean sprouts and cucumber, and stir-fry for an additional 2 minutes. Place the vegetables in a warmed serving dish.

3. To make the peanut sauce add the 2 tbsps oil to the wok and fry the peanuts for 2-3 minutes. Remove and drain on kitchen paper.

4. Blend or pound the chillies, shallots and garlic to a smooth paste. Grind the peanuts to a powder.

5. Heat the wok again and fry the chilli paste in the remaining oil for 2 minutes. Add water and bring to the boil.

6. Add the peanuts, brown sugar, lemon juice and salt. Stir until the sauce is thick, about 10 minutes.

7. Add the coconut milk and stir to blend in evenly. Garnish the vegetable dish with sliced hard-boiled egg and the cucumber, and serve with the peanut sauce.

TIME: Preparation takes about 20 minutes and cooking takes 20 minutes.

BEEF AND SPRING ONION ROLLS

*Slices of beef rolled round spring onions and coated with a well flavoured sauce
make a delicious starter.*

SERVES 4

4-6 spring onions, trimmed and cut into
   5cm/2-inch lengths
120g/4oz sirloin, fat trimmed, sliced very
   thin and cut into 12 × 5cm/5- × 2-inch
   pieces
1 tbsp oil
2 tbsps soy sauce
1 tbsp sugar
1 tbsp saké
1 tbsp dashi
1 tbsp mirin

1. Divide onions equally into as many
groups as you have slices of beef. Roll 1
slice of beef around 1 group of onions.

2. Tie the roll with string. Repeat with
remaining onions and beef.

3. Heat oil in a large heavy-based frying
pan.

4. Add the beef rolls, seam side down, and
cook for about 1 minute over a moderate
heat.

5. Turn the rolls several times to brown
evenly. Reduce the heat and add all remaining ingredients except the mirin and
garnish.

6. Cook a further 3 minutes and remove the
meat with a slotted spoon.

7. Turn up the heat and cook the pan juices
to reduce by half. Add the mirin.

8. Remove the string from the rolls and
return them to the pan. Cook the rolls, turning them often, until well glazed.

9. Cut each roll into 1.25cm/½-inch thick
rounds. Thread the rounds on skewers and
garnish.

TIME: Preparation takes 15 minutes and cooking takes 12-15 minutes.

MUSSELS IN CHILLI SAUCE

Seafood is an important part of the diet in Thailand; here mussels are served in a simple chilli sauce.

SERVES 4

900g/2lbs mussels

280ml/½ pint water

1 stem fresh lemon grass, peeled and the core finely chopped

2.5cm/1-inch piece root ginger, peeled and sliced

4 dried Kaffir lime leaves, crushed

Basil leaves and chilli 'flowers' to garnish

Chilli Sauce

3 large red chillies, chopped

1 tbsp chopped coriander root and stem

2 cloves garlic, crushed

2 tbsps oil

2 tbsps fish sauce

1 tbsp sugar

1 tbsp chopped fresh basil

2 tsps cornflour mixed with a little water

1. Scrub the mussels and remove the beards, discarding any mussels that are open.

2. Bring the water to the boil and add the lemon grass, ginger and lime leaves. Add the mussels, reduce heat and simmer for 10 minutes.

3. Drain the mussels reserving 140ml/¼ pint of the cooking liquid. Discard any mussels that do not open.

4. While the mussels are cooking start to prepare the sauce. Pound the chillies, coriander and garlic together in a pestle and mortar.

5. Heat the oil in a wok and fry the chilli mixture for a few minutes, then stir in the fish sauce, sugar and basil.

6. Add the reserved cooking liquid, then the cornflour mixture, and cook until slightly thickened.

7. Serve the mussels with the sauce poured over them. Garnish with basil leaves and chilli 'flowers'.

TIME: Preparation takes 10 minutes and cooking takes 10 minutes.

PREPARATION: To make chilli 'flowers', slit the chillies at intervals, down to the point, keeping the stem end intact. Scrape out the seeds and put the chillies in iced water for 1-2 hours or until the ends curl outwards to form petals.

VARIATION: Kaffir lime leaves are available in Oriental stores, but lemon grass and fish sauce can also be found at some large supermarkets. If unavailable substitute grated zest of 1 lemon and 2 limes; and 1 tbsp each of anchovy paste and light soy, blended together for the fish sauce.

SWEET AND SOUR FISH SATAY

Monkfish is a lovely firm fleshed 'meaty' fish which is ideal for satays.

SERVES 4

900g/2lbs monkfish
1 medium onion, finely chopped
1 clove garlic, crushed
1 tsp ground coriander
1 tsp grated ginger
3 tbsps dark soy sauce
Juice of 1 lime
2 tsps dark brown sugar
Freshly ground black pepper

1. Cut the fish into 2.5cm/1-inch cubes, removing any skin and bone.

2. Thread the cubes onto skewers and place on a flat plate.

3. Mix the onion, garlic, coriander, ginger, soy sauce, lime juice and sugar in a food processor, blender, or mortar and pestle and work until smooth.

4. Add the black pepper and then spread the mixture over the satays.

5. Turn the skewers to coat the fish evenly and leave for about 1 hour, turning now and again.

6. Cook the fish on a barbecue or under a grill for about 5-10 minutes or until the fish is cooked. Baste with any remaining marinade while cooking.

TIME: Preparation takes about 15 minutes, plus 1 hour marinating; cooking takes between 5 and 10 minutes depending on the power of the grill that is used.

VARIATION: Substitute any other firm-fleshed white fish or try king prawns, and alter cooking time accordingly.

CELLOPHANE NOODLES WITH PRAWNS

An oyster and wine sauce enhances this light and tasty seafood dish.

SERVES 4

250g/9oz cellophane noodles
1 spring onion
1 tbsp oil
24 fresh prawns, peeled
1 tbsp Chinese wine
2 tbsps light soy sauce
½ tsp sugar
1 tbsp oyster sauce
60ml/2 fl oz fish stock
Few drops sesame oil

1. Cook the noodles in boiling, salted water for 1 minute. Drain and rinse under cold water. Set aside to drain.

2. Slice the spring onion into thin rounds. Heat the oil in a wok and stir-fry the spring onion and the prawns for 1 minute.

3. Reduce the heat, drain off the excess fat, and deglaze the wok with the Chinese wine.

4. Stir in the drained noodles, soy sauce, sugar, oyster sauce, fish stock and sesame oil.

5. Cook until the noodles are heated through and then serve immediately.

TIME: Preparation takes about 15 minutes and cooking takes about 8-10 minutes.

VARIATION: The fresh prawns could be replaced with cooked ones.

CHECKPOINT: When adding the noodles to the wok, the heat must be reduced considerably, or the noodles will be overcooked.

SOUR FRIED SEAFOOD

Choose your favourite seafood to make this delicious recipe with.

SERVES 4

450g/1lb mix of the following:
King prawns
Scallops
Squid, cleaned and cut into rings
Oysters, shelled
Clams, shelled
Crab claws, shelled
Small fish such as whitebait or smelt

140ml/¼ pint oil
4 shallots, finely chopped
1 tbsp grated ginger
3 cloves garlic, crushed
4 red chillies, seeded and finely chopped
1 tsp ground mace
½ tsp shrimp paste
1 piece tamarind, soaked in 60ml/4 tbsps
   boiling water
Pinch brown sugar
Salt

1. Heat the oil in a frying pan or wok and when hot add the fish and shellfish and fry for 2-3 minutes or until lightly browned.

2. Cook in 2 or 3 batches. Drain on kitchen paper and set aside.

3. Grind the shallots, ginger, garlic, chillies and mace to a smooth paste in a blender, food processor or mortar and pestle. Add the shrimp paste and blend well.

4. Pour off all but 1 tbsp of the oil from the wok and add the spice paste.

5. Cook gently for 2-3 minutes, then strain in the tamarind water.

6. If the sauce is too thick, add more water to bring to thin coating consistency.

7. Stir in the sugar and salt and add the fish. Cook a further 2 minutes to heat the fish through.

TIME: Preparation takes 15 minutes and cooking takes 10-12 minutes.

VARIATION: If shrimp paste and tamarind are unavailable, substitute anchovy paste and lemon juice.

BALINESE FISH

A tempting combination of lemon grass, ginger and chilli transforms fish steaks into something a bit special.

SERVES 4

2 tbsps oil
90g/3oz finely chopped red onion
2 cloves garlic, finely chopped
2 red or green chillies, finely chopped
1 piece grated ginger
1 tbsp ground turmeric
1 piece lemon grass, peeled and the core
    finely chopped
1 tbsp trassie or anchovy essence
140ml/¼ pint water
4 fish steaks, such as cod, halibut, turbot

1. Heat the oil in a wok or frying pan.

2. Grind the onion, garlic, chillies, ginger, turmeric and lemon grass together with a mortar and pestle and fry them in the oil.

3. Add the trassie and water and bring to the boil.

4. Lower the heat and add the fish steaks. Cover the pan and cook gently for about 15 minutes, or until the fish is completely cooked.

5. Remove the fish from the liquid and boil the sauce rapidly to reduce it.

6. Pour the sauce over the fish to serve.

TIME: Preparation takes about 15 minutes and cooking takes about 20 minutes.

BUYING GUIDE: Trassie is the Indonesian name for shrimp paste; a strong seasoning made from dried salted shrimps. (Also known as Kapi or Blanchan)

ONION FISH

Fish cooked in coconut milk and flavoured with ginger, chillies and lemon makes a delicious combination.

SERVES 4

Grated flesh of 1 coconut
900g/2lbs fish fillets, such as sole or plaice
12 small onions
1 tbsp oil
2 chillies, finely chopped
1 piece ginger, grated
1 tbsp shrimp paste or anchovy essence
Juice and grated rind of 1 lemon
2 curry leaves or bay leaves
Salt and pepper

1. Soak the coconut in one and a half times its volume of tepid water for 15 minutes. Mix well and strain through muslin, squeezing all the liquid out.

2. Wash the fish fillets, pat dry and set aside. Peel the onions but leave them whole.

3. Heat the oil in a frying pan or wok and add the onions, chillies and ginger.

4. Cook for about 1 minute and then add the shrimp paste, the lemon juice and rind, curry leaves or bay leaves and coconut milk.

5. Bring to the boil, and then reduce the heat and cook until the sauce thickens slightly.

6. Add the fish fillets and cook gently until the fish is done. Remove the fish to a serving dish and spoon over some of the sauce.

TIME: Preparation takes about 25 minutes and cooking takes 15-20 minutes.

PREPARATION: To make peeling the onions easy, drop them into boiling water for a minute or two.

SERVING IDEAS: Serve the remaining sauce separately and accompany with rice. Garnish with some curls of fresh coconut if wished.

TAMARIND CHICKEN SATAY

Serve these satays on a bed of rice and accompany with the tomato and chilli sambal to make a main course dish.

SERVES 4

4 chicken breasts, skinned and boned and cut into 1.25cm/½-inch cubes

Marinade
1 tbsp oil
5cm/2-inch piece tamarind soaked in 120ml/4 fl oz hot water
2 cloves garlic, crushed
1 tsp ground cardamom
½ tsp ground nutmeg
Pinch salt and pepper
1 tsp kecap manis

Tomato and chilli sambal
2 red chillies
1 small piece fresh ginger, grated
1 clove garlic, crushed
450g/1lb fresh tomatoes, skinned and seeded
60ml/4 tbsps oil
1 tbsp lemon or lime juice
1 tbsp dark brown sugar

1. Place the chicken in a large bowl and mix the marinade ingredients together. Pour the marinade over the chicken and stir well. Leave in the refrigerator for 30 minutes.

2. Thread the chicken cubes onto thin bamboo skewers.

3. Place the satay on a barbecue grill or under a pre-heated grill. Turn frequently and cook for about 8-10 minutes or until golden brown.

4. During cooking brush the chicken with the remaining marinade.

5. While the chicken is cooking prepare the sambal. Put the chillies, ginger and garlic into a blender or food processor.

6. Add 1 or 2 of the tomatoes and process until the mixture is a smooth paste.

7. Add the remaining tomatoes and process once or twice so that the tomatoes begin to break up but are still in chunks.

8. Heat the oil in a frying pan and fry the tomato sauce for about 5-7 minutes, adding lemon or lime juice.

9. If the sauce gets too thick add a spoonful of water. Stir in the sugar and add salt to taste.

TIME: Preparation takes 30 minutes, including marinating; cooking takes about 10-12 minutes.

COOK'S TIP: Remove the chilli seeds if a milder sambal is required.

BUYING GUIDE: Kecap manis is an Indonesian sauce based on dark soy sauce, sugar and spices.

CHICKEN BREASTS WITH SPRING ONION

Stuffed chicken breasts, steamed and served in a light soy-based sauce.

SERVES 4

---

1 spring onion, cut into rounds
1 carrot, cut into thin julienne
1 tsp chopped garlic
4 chicken breasts
Salt and pepper
175ml/6 fl oz chicken stock
1 tbsp soy sauce
½ tsp sugar
1 tsp cornflour, combined with a little water

---

1. Mix together the spring onion, carrot and half the garlic.

2. Slice the chicken breasts open horizontally, along the length, without cutting through them completely.

3. Season the insides with salt and pepper and cover each breast with ¼ of the vegetable stuffing.

4. Pull the top half of the breast back into place. Season with salt and pepper. Steam for about 15 minutes until cooked through.

5. Meanwhile bring the stock to the boil in a small saucepan. Stir in the soy sauce, sugar and the remaining garlic, simmer and allow to reduce for a few minutes.

6. Thicken the sauce by adding the dissolved cornflour and stirring continuously until the sauce is slightly thickened and glossy.

7. Cut the stuffed chicken breasts into slices and serve them topped with the sauce.

TIME: Preparation takes about 10 minutes and cooking takes about 15 minutes.

SERVING IDEAS: Serve with plain boiled or steamed rice, garnished with 1 tbsp chopped fresh chives.

WATCHPOINT: The spring onion and the carrot must be cut very thinly in order that they cook quickly during steaming.

Noodles with Chicken and Prawns

This is a very quick and simple dish to prepare which can be on the table in about half an hour.

SERVES 4

225g/8oz Chinese noodles

3 tbsps oil

2 shallots, finely chopped

1 clove garlic, crushed

225g/8oz chicken, skinned, boned and cut into small pieces

2 courgettes, cut in strips

3 tbsps soy sauce

60g/2oz cooked, peeled prawns

Salt and pepper

4 spring onions, finely shredded and 1 red chilli, seeded and thinly shredded to garnish

1. Cook the noodles in boiling salted water until just tender.

2. Drain and rinse under hot water and toss in a colander to remove excess water.

3. Heat the oil in a wok or heavy-based frying pan and cook the shallots and garlic until softened.

4. Add the chicken and stir-fry until cooked and the shallots and garlic are lightly browned.

5. Add the courgettes and stir-fry for 1-2 minutes.

6. Add the drained noodles and cook 2-3 minutes.

7. Add the soy sauce and prawns, season with salt and pepper and cook to heat through.

8. Serve garnished with the spring onions and chilli.

TIME: Preparation takes 15 minutes and cooking takes 10-12 minutes.

BUYING GUIDE: Buy the egg noodles that just need very brief cooking in boiling water.

MARINATED FRIED CHICKEN

Kecap manis is an Indonesian thick sweet sauce based on dark soy, sugar and spices; and sambal ulek is a blend of ground red chillies and salt. Both can be used as a seasoning or condiment and are available in Oriental stores.

SERVES 4

Marinade

1 tbsp kecap manis

1 tbsp sambal ulek

2 cloves garlic, crushed

2 shallots, finely chopped

2 tsps chopped fresh coriander leaves

½ tsp ground cumin

3 tbsps oil

Juice of 1 lime or lemon

Salt and pepper

900g-1.4kg/2-3lbs small chicken pieces

90ml/6 tbsps oil

280ml/½ pint coconut milk

Chilli 'flowers' to garnish

1. Combine all of the marinade ingredients in a large bowl.

2. Put in the chicken pieces and turn to coat well. Leave to marinate for 1 hour in the refrigerator.

3. Heat the oil in a wok or large frying pan.

4. When hot, scrape most of the marinade off the pieces of chicken and put them in the hot oil. Cook on both sides to brown quickly.

5. Lower the temperature, cover the wok or frying pan and allow the chicken to cook and brown slowly, for about 45 minutes.

6. Remove the chicken from the wok or frying pan and drain. Discard the oil.

7. Return the chicken to the pan and pour over any remaining marinade.

8. Add the coconut milk and bring to the boil. Turn the chicken over frequently in the sauce, for about 10 minutes, to heat through.

9. Serve garnished with chilli 'flowers'.

TIME: Preparation takes 1 hour, including marinating time; cooking takes about 55 minutes.

PREPARATION: To make chilli 'flowers', cut the chilli at close intervals from stem to tip into thin strips, leaving the stalk and the stem end intact. Leave to stand in iced water until the chilli opens out into a 'flower'.

CHICKEN IN GREEN CHILLI SAUCE

Lemon grass and tamarind combined with spices and peanuts make an excellent sauce for this chicken dish.

SERVES 4

2 green chillies, seeded and chopped
2 green peppers, chopped
60g/2oz raw peanuts
3 tbsps oil
2 onions, finely chopped
2-3 cloves of garlic, crushed
2 tsps fresh ginger, grated
½ tsp ground turmeric
1 piece lemon grass, peeled and core chopped
1 piece tamarind, soaked in 3 tbsps hot water
1.4kg/3lbs chicken pieces
1 curry leaf or bay leaf
Salt
430ml/¾ pint water mixed with the juice of 1 lime
6 spring onions, shredded and roasted peanuts, roughly chopped to garnish

1. Combine the chillies, green peppers and peanuts in a blender or food processor and work to a smooth paste, adding some of the water from the rceipe if necessary.

2. Heat the oil in a wok or large frying pan and add the onions and garlic and sauté slowly until lightly browned.

3. Add the pepper and peanut paste and cook for about 1 minute.

4. Add the ginger, turmeric, lemon grass, the strained liquid from the tamarind, and the chicken pieces.

5. Add the curry leaf or bay leaf and a pinch of salt and gradually pour on the water.

6. Cover the pan or wok and bring the mixture to the boil. Reduce the heat and simmer gently for 45 minutes.

7. Remove the lid, increase the heat and allow the sauce to boil for about 10 minutes, stirring occasionally to reduce the amount of liquid, if necessary.

8. Remove the bay leaf and serve the chicken garnished with spring onion and chopped peanuts, spooning over the sauce.

TIME: Preparation takes 30 minutes and cooking takes about 55 minutes.

VARIATION: Use cashew nuts instead of peanuts.

BRAISED CHICKEN WITH GINGER

In this recipe, boned chicken is coated with ginger and cooked in a vegetable and ginger-flavoured stock.

SERVES 4

---

1 boned chicken, bones reserved
½ tsp chopped fresh ginger root
1 carrot, cut into small cubes
1 turnip, cut into small cubes
1 courgette, cut into small cubes
1 onion, thinly sliced
5 slices fresh root ginger
Salt and pepper

---

1. Separate the breast and the leg meat from the boned chicken. Keep each leg in one piece.

2. Place the remaining meat and the bones from the chicken in a saucepan, with just enough water to cover. Boil until the liquid has reduced to a quarter. Strain the stock through a fine sieve.

3. Sprinkle the chopped ginger on the inside of the 2 pieces of leg meat and season with salt and pepper. Roll up tightly and secure with kitchen string.

4. Add 140ml/¼ pint water to the stock and bring to the boil in a saucepan.

5. Add the prepared vegetables, sliced ginger, rolled leg meat and the 2 breasts. Cook for approximately 35 minutes or until the chicken is cooked through.

6. Take out the rolled leg meat, cut off the string and cut the meat into rounds. Spread the slices on a warmed serving plate.

7. Take out the chicken breasts and slice them thinly. Arrange the slices on the warmed plate with the leg meat. Remove the vegetables using a slotted spoon, arrange them around the meat and then pour over a little of the stock.

8. Serve piping hot.

TIME: Preparation takes about 20 minutes and cooking takes approximately 1 hour.

VARIATION: If you do not want to use the chicken for the stock, use a stock cube dissolved in water.

COOK'S TIP: If you are short of time, do not bone the legs, but simply cut slits in the meat and place the ginger in the slits.

CHICKEN WITH BAMBOO SHOOTS

Quick-fried chicken and bamboo shoots, served in a light ginger and oyster sauce.

SERVES 4

225g/8oz whole bamboo shoots or canned, sliced bamboo shoots

1 tbsp sesame oil

1 chicken, boned and the meat cut into thin slices

1 tsp chopped garlic

½ tsp chopped fresh ginger root

1 tbsp Shaohsing wine

1 tbsp oyster sauce

280ml/½ pint chicken stock

Salt and pepper

1 tsp cornflour, combined with a little water

1. Cut the bamboo shoots in half lengthwise and then cut into thin, half-moonshaped slices.

2. Blanch the slices of bamboo shoot in boiling water, drain and rinse in cold water. Set aside to drain thoroughly.

3. Heat the sesame oil in a wok and stir-fry the chicken, garlic and ginger.

4. Pour off any excess fat. Deglaze the wok with the wine.

5. Stir in the oyster sauce and the stock.

6. Add the bamboo shoots, season with salt and pepper and cook for 2 minutes.

7. Thicken the sauce by stirring in the cornflour and stirring continuously until the sauce reaches the desired consistency. Serve hot.

TIME: Preparation takes about 20 minutes and cooking takes 8-10 minutes.

COOK'S TIP: Sesame oil gives a very strong flavour to this dish, so use half peanut oil and half sesame oil, if preferred.

VARIATION: Shaohsing wine is Chinese rice wine, if unavailable, use dry sherry instead.

LACQUERED 'PEKING' DUCK

These duck breasts are marinated in honey and soy sauce for 24 hours before being baked in the oven.

SERVES 4

½ tsp soy sauce
1 tbsp honey
1 tsp five-spice powder
1 tsp wine vinegar
1 tsp chopped garlic
1 tsp cornflour, combined with a little water
2 duck breasts
Salt and pepper

1. To make the marinade, mix together the soy sauce and the honey.

2. Sprinkle over the five-spice powder and stir in well.

3. Stir in the vinegar, garlic and cornflour.

4. Season the breasts with a little salt and pepper and place in an ovenproof dish. Pour the marinade over to coat the duck breasts entirely. Leave to marinate for 24 hours.

5. Cook the breasts in a hot oven, 220°C/425°F/Gas Mark 7, for approximately 20 minutes, basting frequently with the marinade.

6. To caramelize the tops, put under a hot grill for several minutes until crisp. Watch carefully to prevent them burning.

TIME: Marinating takes 24 hours, preparation takes about 5 minutes and cooking takes approximately 25 minutes.

COOK'S TIP: Start cooking the duck breasts skin side up, and turn them over during cooking. Turn again to glaze the skin side under a hot grill, before serving.

SERVING IDEAS: To serve more people, make twice as much marinade and use a whole duck. Score the skin for the marinade to penetrate and cook the duck in the oven for about 45 minutes – 1 hour.

MAKKHANI MURGHI

Makkhani Murghi, or Chicken in a Butter Sauce, is rich, delicious and irresistible! It is bound to be an overwhelming success with your dinner guests!

SERVES 6-8

1kg/2¼lbs chicken breast, skinned
1¼ tsps salt or to taste
2.5cm/1-inch cube of fresh root ginger, peeled and coarsely chopped
4-6 cloves garlic, coarsely chopped
150g/5oz thick set natural yogurt
The juice of 1 lemon

Grind the following 5 ingredients in a coffee grinder
1 cinnamon stick, 5cm/2-inches long; broken up
8 green cardamoms with the skin
6 whole cloves
8-10 red chillies
6-8 white peppercorns

2 tbsps cooking oil
2 tbsps tomato purée
225g/8oz butter
400g/14oz can of tomatoes
2 cinnamon sticks, each 5cm/2-inches long; broken up
140ml/5 fl oz single cream

1. Wash and dry the chicken and cut into 10 × 5cm/4 × 2-inch strips.

2. Add the salt to the ginger and garlic and crush to a smooth pulp.

3. Combine the yogurt, lemon juice and the ground spices and beat until the mixture is smooth. Marinate the chicken in this mixture, cover the container and leave for 4 hours or overnight in the refrigerator.

4. Heat the oil over medium heat and add the ginger/garlic pulp, stir and fry for 1 minute. Add the chicken and stir and fry for 10 minutes.

5. Add the tomato purée and butter, cook on low heat, uncovered, for 10 minutes. Remove the pan from the heat, cover and keep aside.

6. Put the tomatoes and the cinnamon sticks in a separate pan, bring to the boil, cover and simmer for 10 minutes. Remove the lid and adjust heat to medium; cook uncovered until the liquid is reduced to half its original volume (6-8 minutes). Remove the pan from the heat and allow the tomato mixture to cool slightly.

7. Sieve the cooked tomatoes, discard the cinnamon sticks. Add the sieved tomatoes to the chicken and place the pan over medium heat. Bring the liquid to the boil, reduce heat to low and cook, uncovered, for 5-6 minutes.

8. Add the cream, stir and mix well, and simmer uncovered for about 5 minutes. Remove from the heat.

TIME: Preparation takes 20-25 minutes plus at least 4 hours marinating, cooking takes 40-45 minutes.

SERVING IDEAS: Serve with Naan bread or plain boiled rice.

PORK WRAPPED IN NOODLES

Relatively mild in flavour, these crisp balls are served with a hot dipping sauce.

SERVES 4

225g/8oz minced pork
1 tsp ground coriander
1 tbsp fish sauce
1 small egg, beaten
90g/3oz rice noodles (vermicelli)
Oil for deep frying

Whole chillies to garnish

Nam Prik Sauce
1 tsp shrimp paste
1 tsp salt
1 tsp light brown sugar
4 cloves garlic, crushed
5 small red chillies, chopped
8 anchovy fillets, chopped
1 tbsp light soy sauce
Juice of ½ lime

1. Mix together the pork, coriander and fish sauce until well combined, then add enough egg to bind.

2. Roll the pork into small balls and chill for 30 minutes.

3. Cover the noodles with warm water and soak for about 10 minutes to soften.

4. Pound together the shrimp paste, salt, sugar, garlic, chillies and anchovies to a smooth paste in a pestle and mortar or mini food processor. Stir in the soy sauce and lime juice and transfer to a small serving dish.

5. Drain the noodles then wrap several strands around each pork ball.

6. Heat the oil for deep frying in a wok and fry a few at a time for 3-4 minutes or until crisp and golden. Drain on kitchen paper and keep hot until all are cooked.

7. Serve immediately with the dipping sauce and garnish with whole chillies.

TIME: Preparation takes 20 minutes, plus chilling cooking takes about 20 minutes.

VARIATION: Use 2 extra anchovy fillets if shrimp paste is unavailable. Chilli seeds can be removed to make a milder sauce.

BUYING GUIDE: Shrimp paste, also known as shrimp sauce can be bought in Oriental stores. Fish sauce and rice noodles are now also available in some supermarkets.

RICE-COATED MEATBALLS

These highly seasoned meatballs, coated in pre-soaked rice, could also be made using any type of meat.

SERVES 4

120g/4oz long grain rice, pre-soaked in
    warm water for 2 hours
630g/1lb 6oz boned pork shoulder, minced
2.5cm/1-inch piece fresh ginger root,
    peeled and chopped
½ tsp shallots, finely chopped
½ tsp finely chopped fresh parsley
½ tsp finely chopped fresh chives
½ tsp soy sauce
½ egg, beaten
Tip of a knife of chilli sauce
Salt and pepper

1. Mix together the meat, ginger, shallots, parsley, chives, soy sauce, egg and chilli sauce. Beat well to combine all the ingredients.

2. Season with salt and pepper and then form into small meat balls.

3. Drain the rice very carefully, shaking well to remove all the water. Spread the rice on your work surface.

4. Roll the meat balls in the rice to coat them evenly.

5. Steam the meat balls for approximately 15 minutes. The exact cooking time will depend on the thickness of your meatballs, but small ones take 15 minutes.

TIME: Pre-soaking the rice takes 2 hours, preparation takes about 30 minutes and cooking takes approximately 15-20 minutes if you can steam all the meat balls in one batch, longer if you need to do two batches.

COOK'S TIP: Rinse your hands in cold water before shaping the meat balls, otherwise they tend to stick and break up.

VARIATION: Any type of meat can be used for these meat balls, so try beef, veal or even chicken.

STIR-FRIED BEEF WITH PINEAPPLE

Sliced fillet steak cooked with fresh pineapple and served in a sweet, pungent sauce makes a delicious dish.

SERVES 4

450g/1lb fillet steak
½ fresh pineapple
1 tbsp oil
1 spring onion, chopped
½ tsp chopped fresh root ginger
1 tsp vinegar
1 tsp sugar
2 tsps light soy sauce
280ml/½ pint chicken stock
120ml/4 fl oz pineapple juice
½ tomato, seeded and chopped
1 tsp cornflour, combined with a little water
Salt and pepper

1. Cut the fillet steak into thin strips and season with salt and pepper.

2. Cut the skin off the pineapple and cut out all the brown 'eyes' from the flesh.

3. Cut into round slices, removing any tough parts and the core.

4. Cut the remaining flesh into small, even pieces.

5. Heat the oil in the wok. Add the onion, ginger and the meat and stir-fry until lightly coloured.

6. Pour off any excess fat.

7. Stir in the vinegar, sugar, soy sauce, chicken stock and pineapple juice. Add the tomato and the pineapple pieces. Reduce the heat and cook for a few minutes.

8. Add the cornflour gradually, stirring continuously until the sauce is thickened and glossy.

TIME: Preparation takes about 15 minutes and cooking takes about 8-10 minutes.

VARIATION: Fresh pineapple juice could be used. Liquidize the remaining ½ pineapple and then pass it through a sieve. Make up to 100ml/4 fl oz with water if necessary.

STIR-FRIED PORK AND VEGETABLES

A quick and easy stir-fry of pork, bean sprouts and carrot, served in a spicy, slightly sweet sauce.

SERVES 4

1 carrot, cut into thin matchsticks
225g/8oz bean sprouts
2 tbsps oil
Slice of fresh ginger root
1 spring onion, chopped
½ tsp chopped garlic
450g/1lb pork, cut into thin slices
2 tsps sake
300ml/½ pint chicken stock
Salt and pepper
½ tsp brown sugar
1 tsp cornflour, combined with a little water

1. In a small saucepan, bring to the boil a little salted water. Blanch the julienned carrot in this water for 1 minute. Drain well, reserving the water.

2. Wash the bean sprouts in lots of running water and blanch for 1 minute in the water used for the carrot. Rinse well and drain.

3. Heat the oil in a wok. Stir-fry the ginger, spring onion and the garlic until slightly coloured.

4. Add the meat, stir in well and cook for 1 minute.

5. Add the well-drained vegetables, wine and stock. Season with salt and pepper, stir together well and cook for 2 minutes.

6. Add the sugar to the contents of the wok and thicken the sauce with the cornflour, adding it gradually and stirring continuously until the desired consistency is reached. Remove the ginger before serving.

TIME: Preparation takes about 25 minutes and cooking takes approximately 10 minutes.

SERVING IDEAS: Sprinkle a few drops of sesame oil over the finished dish.

COOK'S TIP: Stir-fry the spring onion and the ginger before the chopped garlic, as the garlic tends to stick and brown before the spring onion is cooked.

BEEF WITH CHINESE MUSHROOMS

Unlike most Chinese meat dishes, this one does not have a sauce. The beef is first marinated and then simply dry-cooked with the mushrooms.

SERVES 4

1 tsp cornflour
1 tbsp light soy sauce
1 egg white
1 tsp sugar
450g/1lb rump steak, thinly sliced
6 dried Chinese black mushrooms
2 tbsps oil
½ tsp chopped garlic
Salt and pepper
2 tbsps Chinese wine

1. To make the marinade, place the cornflour in a bowl and stir in the soy sauce. Beat in the egg white and the sugar, beating thoroughly to combine all the ingredients. Add the slices of beef and leave to marinate for 1 hour.

2. Meanwhile, soak the mushrooms in warm water for 1 hour, then drain them, and cut into thin strips.

3. Heat the oil in a wok, stir-fry the garlic, beef and the mushrooms until coloured and the meat tender. Season with salt and pepper.

4. Stir in the wine and serve as soon as it has evaporated.

TIME: Preparation takes about 10 minutes, plus 1 hour marinating; and cooking takes approximately 8-10 minutes.

SERVING IDEAS: Serve with plain steamed rice or stir-fried rice and vegetables.

FIVE SPICE PORK

Serve this delicious, sweet, spicy dish with rice.

SERVES 4

675g/1½lb belly of pork strips
2 tbsps oil
1 tbsp curry paste
2 tbsps fish sauce
1 tbsp light soy sauce
2 tbsps sugar
1 tsp five spice powder
1 tbsp chopped fresh lemon grass (soft core
    only), or 1½ tsps dried

Fresh coriander and lime twists to garnish

1. Cut the pork strips into 4cm/1½-inch chunks.

2. Heat the oil in a wok and fry the curry paste for 2 minutes, stir in the fish sauce, soy sauce, sugar, five spice powder and lemon grass. Cook for a further 3 minutes.

3. Add the pork to the wok and cook, tossing frequently for 10 minutes until the pork is cooked.

4. Serve garnished with fresh coriander and lime twists.

TIME: Preparation takes 10 minutes and cooking takes 15 minutes.

PREPARATION: To prepare the fresh lemon grass, peel off the tough outside leaves and dry top portions, then chop the soft interior.

BUYING GUIDE: Fish sauce can be bought at Oriental stores and some supermarkets. If unavailable, mix together equal quantities of anchovy paste and light soy sauce.

Kheema Mattar

A popular dish all over India, especially in the north. Lean mince is combined with garden peas and ground almonds and garnished with sliced hard-boiled eggs to make an attractive and delicious dish.

SERVES 4

90ml/6 tbsps cooking oil
1 tsp cumin seeds
2 dried red chillies
450g/1lb lean mince, lamb or beef
1 large onion, finely chopped
2.5cm/1-inch cube of fresh root ginger,
  peeled and finely grated
4 cloves garlic, crushed
½ tsp ground turmeric
2 tsps ground coriander
1½ tsps ground cumin
½ tsp chilli powder
1 small can of tomatoes or 3-4 fresh
  tomatoes, skinned and chopped
1 tsp salt
180ml/6 fl oz warm water
1 tbsp natural yogurt
120g/4oz fresh or frozen garden peas;
  shelled weight
1 tbsp ground almonds
½ garam masala
2 hard-boiled eggs, sliced
2 tbsps chopped coriander leaves to
  garnish

1. Heat 1 tbsp oil over medium heat and add the cumin seeds, as soon as they pop add the red chillies and then the mince. Stir and cook until the mince is evenly browned.

2. Meanwhile, heat the remaining oil over a medium heat and add the onions. Stir and fry until the onions are soft, add the ginger and garlic and stir and fry for a further 2-3 minutes.

3. Stir in the turmeric and then the coriander, cumin and chilli powder.

4. Add the tomatoes along with all the juice, stir and cook for 3-4 minutes.

5. Add the mince and cook for 6-8 minutes, stirring frequently.

6. Add the salt and water and stir in the yogurt.

7. Cover the pan and simmer for 20 minutes.

8. Add the frozen peas and simmer for a further 10 minutes. If using fresh peas, boil until tender before adding to the mince.

9. Stir in the ground almonds and simmer for 2-3 minutes.

10. Remove from heat and stir in the garam masala.

11. Transfer onto a serving dish and arrange the sliced eggs on top. Garnish with the coriander leaves.

TIME: Preparation takes 15 minutes, cooking takes 50 minutes.

SERVING IDEAS: Serve with chapatties, and/or fried brown rice. Suitable for freezing if fresh peas are used.

VARIATION: Add peeled and diced potatoes in stage 7.

FRAGRANT PINEAPPLE AND COCONUT RICE

This beautifully fragrant rice dish complements any Oriental dish perfectly.

SERVES 4

700ml/1¼ pints coconut milk
Pinch ground clove
½ tsp ground cinnamon
½ ground nutmeg
Pinch cayenne pepper
Grated rind and juice of 1 lemon
1 curry leaf or bay leaf
225g/8oz long grain rice
30g/1oz butter or margarine
1 green pepper, thinly sliced
1 small fresh pineapple, or 225g/8oz canned pineapple, cut into chunks
Salt and pepper

1. Pour the coconut milk into a large, heavy-based saucepan and add all the spices, the lemon rind and juice, and curry leaf or bay leaf. Bring the mixture to the boil, stirring constantly.

2. Add the rice and bring the mixture back just to the boil. Lower the heat, cover the pan and simmer very gently for about 20 minutes.

3. Remove the pan from the heat, stir and leave covered. Leave to stand for 5 minutes.

4. Meanwhile, melt the butter or margarine in a frying pan. Add the pepper and pineapple and stir over high heat until the pineapple browns lightly.

5. Remove the bay leaf from the rice and toss with the pineapple and pepper. Fluff with a fork before serving.

TIME: Preparation takes 15 minutes and cooking takes 25 minutes.

BUYING GUIDE: Coconut milk is available in some supermarkets and all Oriental stores. Instant coconut milk is also available in packets.

POTATOES WITH GARLIC AND CHILLIES

These are rather like spicy French fries, but they are not deep fried. A perfect alternative to chips or French fries when you want a touch of spice with plain meat, fish or chicken.

SERVES 4-6

450g/1lb waxy potatoes, peeled and
    washed
3 tbsps cooking oil
½ tsp black mustard seeds
½ tsp cumin seeds
4 cloves garlic, crushed
¼-½ tsp chilli powder
½ tsp ground turmeric
1 tsp salt

1. Cut the potatoes to the thickness of French fries, but half their length.

2. In a wide, shallow non-stick or cast iron pan, heat the oil over medium heat.

3. Add the mustard seeds and then the cumin. When the seeds start popping, add the garlic and allow it to turn lightly brown.

4. Remove the pan from the heat and add the chilli powder and turmeric.

5. Add the potatoes and place the pan back on the heat. Stir and turn heat up to medium.

6. Add the salt, stir and mix, cover the pan and cook for 3-4 minutes and stir again. Continue to do this until the potatoes are cooked and lightly browned. Remove from the heat.

TIME: Preparation takes 15-20 minutes, cooking takes 15 minutes.

SERVING IDEAS: Serve with any curry and rice or Chapatties/Rotis.

VARIATION: Use cauliflower florets, cut into small pieces.

SPICED LENTILS

Dhal of some sort is always cooked as part of a meal in an Indian household.
As a vast majority of the Indian population is vegetarian, dhal is a good
source of protein.

SERVES 4

175g/6oz Masoor dhal (red split lentils)
700ml/1¼ pints water
1 tsp ground turmeric
1 tsp ground cumin
1 tsp salt
30g/1oz ghee or unsalted butter
1 medium onion, finely chopped
2 cloves garlic, finely chopped
2 dried red chillies, coarsely chopped
    soaked in boiling water for 10 minutes

---

1. Put the dhal, water, turmeric, cumin and salt into a saucepan and bring the liquid to the boil.

2. Reduce heat to medium and cook uncovered for 8-10 minutes, stirring frequently.

3. Now cover the pan and simmer for 30 minutes, stirring occasionally.

4. Remove the dhal from the heat, allow to cool slightly and mash through a sieve.

5. Melt the ghee or butter over a medium heat and fry the onion, garlic and red chillies until the onions are well browned, about 8-10 minutes.

6. Stir in half the fried onion mixture to the dhal and put the dhal in a serving dish. Arrange the remaining fried onions on top.

TIME: Preparation takes about 10 minutes, cooking takes about 50 minutes.

SERVING IDEAS: Serve with plain boiled rice and Makkhani Murghi.

WATCHPOINT: Pulses tend to froth and spill over. The initial cooking without the lid in stage 2 should help to eliminate this problem, but should you find that it is spilling over, then partially cover the pan until the froth settles down; this should take only a few minutes.

Mushroom Pilau

The delicate flavour of the mushrooms blends happily with the distinctive flavour and aroma of basmati rice and the whole spices used in this pilau. Other long grain rice can be used, but the pilau will not be as fragrant and delicious as basmati rice.

SERVES 4-6

280g/10oz basmati rice

60g/2oz ghee or unsalted butter

1 tsp caraway seeds

1 large onion, finely sliced

2 cinnamon sticks, each 5cm/2-inches long; broken up

225g/8oz button mushrooms, thickly sliced

½ tsp ground turmeric

1¼ tsps salt or to taste

500ml/18 fl oz water

6 green cardamoms, split open at the top of each pod

6 whole cloves

2 fresh bay leaves, crumpled

1. Wash and soak the rice in cold water for 30 minutes. Drain and keep aside.

2. Melt the ghee or butter over medium heat and fry the caraway seeds for 30 seconds.

3. Add the onions and cinnamon sticks, stir and fry for about 6-8 minutes, or until the onions are golden brown.

4. Add the rice and fry, stirring constantly, for 3-4 minutes. Add the mushrooms, turmeric and salt, stir and fry for a further 2-3 minutes over a low heat.

5. Add the water, cardamoms, cloves and bay leaves; bring to the boil, cover the pan and simmer for 12-15 minutes. Do not lift the lid or stir the rice during cooking.

6. Remove from the heat, uncover and allow steam to escape for 1-2 minutes. Cover the pan and keep aside for 10-15 minutes before serving.

TIME: Preparation takes 20-25 minutes plus time needed to soak the rice, cooking takes 25-30 minutes.

COOK'S TIP: Remove cinnamon sticks, cardamoms, cloves and bay leaves before serving.

COOKED SALAD WITH COCONUT DRESSING

This salad combines crisp-cooked vegetables with raw and is tossed in a well flavoured coconut sauce.

SERVES 4

450g/1lb, total weight, of the following, mixed:
Aubergine, cubed, salted and left to stand for 30 minutes, rinsed
French beans
Carrots, sliced or cut into strips
Courgettes, sliced or cubed
Red or green pepper, shredded
Spring onions, shredded or sliced
Bean sprouts
Cucumber, peeled, seeded and cubed

Dressing
½ fresh coconut, grated
½ tsp shrimp paste
Juice of ½ lemon
1 clove garlic, crushed
1 tsp brown sugar
1 red or green chilli, seeded and finely chopped
Salt
Watercress to garnish

1. Prepare the vegetables and steam the aubergine and carrots for 10-12 minutes.

2. Steam the beans and courgettes for 4-6 minutes or until crisp-tender.

3. Allow the cooked vegetables to cool and combine with the prepared uncooked vegetables.

4. Combine the coconut with one and a half times its volume of tepid water and soak for 15 minutes. Mix well and strain through muslin, squeezing all the liquid out. Mix this with the remaining dressing ingredients in a blender or food processor until smooth, or use a mortar and pestle.

5. Toss the vegetables with the dressing and serve garnished with watercress.

TIME: Preparation takes 30 minutes and cooking takes 15-20 minutes.

PREPARATION: The exact cooking time will depend on the thickness of the vegetable slices.

CHAPATTIES

A Chapatti is a dry roasted unleavened bread best eaten as soon as it is cooked.
They are not very filling so 2-3 chapatties per person
is quite normal.

MAKES 14 Chapatties

340g/12oz fine wholemeal flour or Atta/
  Chapatti flour
½ tsp salt
1 tbsp ghee or unsalted butter
175ml-280ml/6-10 fl oz warm water
  (quantity depends on the texture of the
  flour)
1 tbsp extra flour in a shallow bowl or plate

1. Food Mixer Method: Place the flour, salt and fat together in the bowl and mix thoroughly at the medium-to-low speed taking care to see that all the fat has been broken up and well incorporated into the flour. Turn speed down to minimum and gradually add the water. When the dough is formed, knead it until it is soft and pliable. Cover the dough with a well-moistened cloth and keep aside for ½-1 hour.

2. Hand Method: Put the flour and salt in a large bowl and rub in the fat. Gradually add the water and keep mixing and kneading until a soft and pliable dough is formed. Cover the dough as above and keep aside.

3. Divide the dough into 14 walnut-sized portions. Roll each portion in a circular motion between the palms to make a smooth round ball, then flatten the ball to make a round cake. Dip each cake into the extra flour and roll the chapatti into a disc of about 6-inch diameter.

4. Heat an iron griddle or heavy based frying pan over medium heat and place a chapatti on it, cook for 30 seconds and turn the chapatti over. Cook until brown spots appear on both sides, turning it over frequently.

5. To keep the chapatties warm, line a piece of aluminium foil with absorbent paper and place the chapatties on one end, cover with the other end and seal the edges.

TIME: Preparation takes 35-45 minutes plus ½-1 hour standing time.
Cooking takes 35-40 minutes.

SERVING IDEAS: Serve with any meat, chicken or vegetable curry.
Suitable for freezing.

WATCHPOINT: Overheating the griddle pan will cause the chapatties to
stick and burn.

STIR-FRIED VEGETABLES

Crispy vegetables cooked with the flavour of lemon and prawns, make an excellent combination.

SERVES 4

2 tbsps oil
½ tsp grated ginger
1 clove garlic, crushed
1 onion, sliced in strips
2 carrots, thinly sliced
60g/2oz broccoli florets, broken into small
   pieces
2 sticks celery, sliced diagonally
1 courgette, diagonally sliced
120g/4oz bean sprouts
1 red pepper, cut into strips
1 stem lemon grass, peeled and the core
   chopped
1 tbsp soy sauce
¼ tsp shrimp paste
Salt and pepper

1. Heat the oil in a wok and add the ginger, garlic, onions, carrots, broccoli and celery, and toss in the oil for 2-3 minutes.

2. Add the courgette, bean sprouts and pepper and cook for 1-2 minutes longer.

3. Add the lemon grass, soy sauce, shrimp paste and salt and pepper.

4. Cook for another 30 seconds and serve immediately.

TIME: Preparation takes about 20 minutes and cooking takes 4-5 minutes.

COOK'S TIP: Make sure all the vegetables are prepared before starting to cook them.

BEAN SPROUT SALAD

A marvellously light and refreshing salad.

SERVES 4

400g/14oz fresh bean sprouts
½ red pepper
1 carrot
½ cucumber
2 slices ham
½ tsp chopped garlic
½ tsp chilli sauce
2 tbsps soy sauce
Salt and pepper
1 tbsp oil
½ tsp sugar
1 drop wine vinegar
1 tbsp crushed tomato
½ tbsp sesame oil

1. Cook the bean sprouts in boiling water for 15 minutes. Refresh in cold water and set aside to drain.

2. Cut the pepper, carrot, cucumber and ham into thin strips.

3. In a bowl, mix together the chopped garlic, chilli sauce, soy sauce, salt, pepper, oil, sugar, vinegar and crushed tomato. Stir together well to make a sauce.

4. Toss together the bean sprouts, vegetables and ham. Pour over the sauce and the sesame oil. Serve chilled.

TIME: Preparation takes about 20 minutes and cooking takes 15 minutes.

SERVING IDEAS: Sprinkle with freshly chopped chives.

COOK'S TIP: If you have not been able to buy fresh bean sprouts, use the canned variety. Rinse them under cold running water and use directly in the salad – there is no need to cook them.

RUJAK

This spiced fruit and vegetable salad, combined with a full-flavoured sauce makes an excellent accompaniment to hot curried dishes.

SERVES 4-6

1 grapefruit
2 green apples, cored but not peeled
1 orange
1 small fresh pineapple, peeled and diced
1 mango, peeled and sliced
1 large cucumber, peeled and diced
1 small bunch radishes, washed, trimmed
    and halved, or sliced if large
½ tsp shrimp paste
1-2 tbsps dark brown sugar
1 tbsp soy sauce
½ tsp chilli powder
2 tbsps lemon juice

1. Peel the grapefruit and segment it, catching the juice in a bowl. Add the segments to the juice.

2. Slice the apples and place in a bowl with the grapefruit juice to keep them white.

3. Segment the orange over the bowl to catch the juice and then add the orange segments.

4. Add the pineapple, mango, cucumber, and radishes to the other ingredients in the bowl. Chill thoroughly.

5. Stir the shrimp paste, brown sugar, soy sauce, chilli powder and lemon juice together and mix well to dissolve the sugar.

6. Add to the salad ingredients and stir well to blend. Serve chilled.

TIME: Preparation takes about 25 minutes plus chilling.

BUYING GUIDE: Shrimp paste, needs storing in an airtight container as its smell is very pungent.

CUCUMBER AND ONION RAITA

Raitas and salads are an integral part of an Indian meal. This raita is particularly easy to make and the roasted cumin seeds add a special flavour.

SERVES 4-6

1 tsp cumin seeds
150g/5oz natural yogurt
3 tbsps finely chopped onions
½ cucumber, peeled and finely chopped
½ tsp salt

1. Heat a cast iron or other heavy-based pan and dry-roast the cumin seeds until they become aromatic. Allow to cool and crush them lightly.

2. Stir the yogurt with a fork until smooth, add the rest of the ingredients and half the crushed cumin seeds. Mix thoroughly.

3. Put the raita in a serving dish and sprinkle the remaining cumin seeds on top.

TIME: Preparation takes 10-15 minutes.

SERVING IDEAS: Serve with any curry, especially suitable to serve with hot chilli laced dishes.

SWEET TEMPURA

Tempura is the Japanese name given to any food that is coated in a light batter.

SERVES 4

Selection of the following prepared as
  directed:
Strawberries, hulled, washed and drained
Kiwi fruit, peeled and cut into 5mm/¼-inch
  slices
Apples, cored and cut into wedges, lightly
  sprinkled with lemon juice
Pears, peeled, cored and cut into wedges,
  lightly sprinkled with lemon juice
Pineapple, peeled, cored and cut in rings or
  pieces
Banana, peeled and sliced, lightly sprinkled
  with lemon juice
Plums, small ones left whole
Tangerine, peeled and segmented
Melon, peeled, seeded and cut into cubes
  or wedges
Oil for deep frying

Batter
1 egg
140ml/¼ pint iced water
90g/3oz plain flour
60g/2oz cornflour

Clear honey

1. Prepare fruit before preparing the batter.

2. Pre-heat oil in a deep-fat fryer or wok to 350°F/180°C.

3. Lightly beat the egg and stir in the water. Sift in the flour and cornflour and stir in with a table knife.

4. Do not overmix; batter should be lumpy and there should be flour lining the sides of the bowl.

5. Dip a few of the prepared fruit into the batter and lower carefully into the hot oil.

6. Cook for 2-3 minutes until lightly golden and crisp. Cook in small batches and cook only one kind of fruit at a time.

7. Drain for a few seconds on kitchen paper. Arrange on serving plates and drizzle with honey. Serve immediately.

TIME: Preparation takes about 20 minutes and cooking takes 2-3 minutes per batch.

COOK'S TIP: The secret of good tempura is to under mix the batter.

SPICED MANGO FOOL

In India, mango is considered to be the king of all fruits. The taste of this tropical fruit, which grows extensively in India, is simply delicious.

SERVES 6-8

2 tbsps milk
¼ tsp saffron strands
175g/6oz evaporated milk
60g/2oz sugar
1 tbsp fine semolina
2 heaped tbsps ground almonds
1 tsp ground cardamom
450g/1lb mango pulp or 2 × 425g/15oz cans
    of mangoes, drained and puréed
250g/9oz fromage frais

1. Put the milk into a small saucepan and bring to the boil. Stir in the saffron strands, remove from the heat, cover the pan and keep aside.

2. Put the evaporated milk and sugar into a saucepan and place it over a low heat.

3. When it begins to bubble, sprinkle the semolina over, stir until well blended.

4. Now add the ground almonds, stir and cook for 5-6 minutes or until the mixture thickens.

5. Stir in the ground cardamom and remove from heat. Allow this to cool completely, then gradually beat in the mango pulp, making sure there are no lumps.

6. In a large mixing bowl gradually stir the evaporated milk and mango mixture into the fromage frais.

7. Stir in the saffron milk along with all the strands as these will continue to impart their colour and flavour into the mango pulp. Mix well, until all is evenly blended.

8. Put the mango fool into a serving dish and chill for 2-3 hours.

TIME: Preparation takes 10 minutes, cooking takes 10-15 minutes. Chill for 2-3 hours before serving.

VARIATION: Top the dessert with a few strawberries for an attractive look.

Banana Coconut Lace Pancakes

Lace-thin pancakes, stuffed with a spiced coconut and banana filling make a delicious combination to end any meal.

SERVES 4

Pancake batter
150g/5oz plain flour
Pinch salt
1 tsp sugar
1 egg, beaten
280ml/½ pint coconut milk
Oil for frying

Filling
4 bananas, peeled and mashed
120g/4oz palm sugar or light brown sugar
1 fresh coconut, grated or 225g/8oz
    desiccated coconut
Pinch ground cinnamon
Pinch ground nutmeg
2 tsps lime or lemon juice
280ml/½ pint water

Desiccated coconut to decorate

1. Sift the flour for the pancakes with the salt and sugar, making a well in the centre. Mix the egg and the coconut milk together and pour into the well in the flour.

2. Beat the egg and milk well, drawing in flour gradually from the sides of the bowl. Beat to a smooth, thin batter.

3. Lightly oil a crêpe pan or small frying pan. Place over high heat and when hot, drizzle the batter into the pan in a thin stream to form a lacy pattern.

4. Cook gently until just pale brown. Turn over and cook until the other side is set. Leave the pancakes stacked up and covered with kitchen paper until ready to use.

5. Make the filling, combine all the ingredients in a small saucepan and heat gently until the sugar has dissolved.

6. Allow to simmer for a few minutes until the coconut has absorbed all the liquid, yet the mixture is still moist.

7. Divide the filling equally among all the pancakes and roll up or fold. Place seam side down on a serving plate and sprinkle the desiccated coconut over to decorate.

TIME: Preparation takes about 30 minutes and cooking takes about 20 minutes.

COOK'S TIP: Make the pancake batter in a food processor or blender for ease.

VARIATION: Use cow's milk for the pancake batter if coconut milk is unavailable.

ORANGE AND KIWI JELLY

This combination of orange and green colours makes a very eye catching dessert.

SERVES 4-6

430ml/¾ pint orange juice
140ml/¼ pint water
120g/4oz sugar
2 tsps agar-agar
1 or 2 kiwi fruit, peeled

---

1. Put orange juice and water into a saucepan and heat until boiling.

2. Remove from the heat and stir in the sugar until dissolved.

3. Sprinkle on the agar-agar and whisk until dissolved.

4. Dampen an 1150ml/2 pint loaf tin and pour in the mixture. Leave in the refrigerator to set. Unmould onto a serving dish. Slice the kiwi fruit and arrange on top of the jelly.

TIME: Preparation takes about 20 minutes, plus setting time.

COOK'S TIP: Use agar-agar like gelatine, it is a vegetable substitute made from seaweed.

Spiced Fruit Salad

This is a fruit salad with a difference, and if presented well will make a spectacular end to a special meal.

SERVES 4-6

1 mango, peeled and sliced

1 small pineapple, skinned, cored and sliced

2 bananas, peeled and sliced

4 rambutans or lychees, peeled

1-2 kiwi fruit, peeled and sliced

1 melon, peeled and sliced

2 oranges, peeled and segmented

120g/4oz palm sugar or light brown sugar

1 tsp tamarind extract mixed with 2 tbsps water

Juice of 1 lime

1 piece fresh ginger, grated

½ tsp ground nutmeg

¼ tsp ground cinnamon

Pinch ground coriander

1. Prepare all the fruit, peeling over a bowl to catch the juice.

2. Arrange the prepared fruit on a serving plate or in a bowl.

3. Combine the sugar, tamarind water, lime juice and spices.

4. Pour over the fruit and chill before serving.

TIME: Preparation takes about 30 minutes plus chilling.

COOK'S TIP: If all the above exotic fruits are unavailable, substitute with other fruit, peeled and sliced.

SERVING IDEAS: Serve with Banana Coconut Lace Pancakes.

Index

OF TIME & PLACE

WALKER EVANS AND WILLIAM CHRISTENBERRY